This book belongs to

Elaine Kazarian

a woman after
God's own heart.
I would hope...

Following God
with All Your Heart

GROWTH AND STUDY GUIDE

Elizabeth George

HARVEST HOUSE PUBLISHERS

EUGENE, OREGON

Cover photo © Thomas Dobner / Alamy; back cover author photo © Harry Langdon

Cover by Dugan Design Group, Bloomington, Minnesota

FOLLOWING GOD WITH ALL YOUR HEART
GROWTH AND STUDY GUIDE

Copyright © 2008 by Elizabeth George
Published by Harvest House Publishers
Eugene, Oregon 97402
www.harvesthousepublishers.com

Library of Congress Cataloging-in-Publication Data

ISBN-13: 978-0-7369-1769-8
ISBN-10: 0-7369-1769-1

Printed in the United States of America

08 09 10 11 12 13 14 15 16 / BP-SK / 10 9 8 7 6 5 4 3 2 1

Contents

Becoming a Contented Woman

Becoming a Confident Woman

1

Success Made Simple

This Book of the Law shall not depart from your mouth,
but you shall meditate in it day and night,
that you may observe to do
according to all that is written in it.
For then you will make your way prosperous,
and then you will have good success.

Joshua 1:8

 Read chapter 1, "Success Made Simple," in *Following God with All Your Heart*. Note any new truths or encouragements that motivate you to tackle what God is asking of you today.

What exciting opportunities are yours today as you seek to follow God? Jot them down and keep them in mind as you work your way through this exciting lesson on trusting God for His will and plan for your life.

Hiding God's Word in Your Heart

Memorize Joshua 1:8. Write down how it appears in your favorite version of the Bible. You may want to look at a few other translations and note any words that differ to help you better understand the meaning of this powerful verse. What part of this verse really stands out and speaks to your heart today?

God Shows You the Way to Success

Using a dictionary, write out a definition of "success."

What does Joshua 1:8 say is involved in success?

A Man Who Wholeheartedly Followed God

Read Joshua 1:1-9. List several things you learn about Joshua in these few verses.

Joshua is a dynamic figure in history. Look up the following verses and jot down the highlights of his life that led up to his encounter with God at the Jordan River.

Exodus 17:8-13—

Exodus 24:13—

Exodus 33:11—

Numbers 13:16-18 and 14:6-9—

Numbers 27:15-22—

A Woman's Heart for God

Every Christian woman has many roles and responsibilities along with nurturing her relationship with the Lord. What are your daily responsibilities at this stage of your life? And what does God expect you to take care of, regardless of the challenges? List your job assignments from God.

Joshua was given the job of shepherding God's people. What similarities do you see between your God-given responsibilities and Joshua's?

Look in your book at the three instances where God told Joshua to be strong and courageous. Note the golden promise God added in each case:

Joshua 1:6—

verse 7—

verse 9—

Pinpoint a hurdle in front of you. Share in a sentence how God's commands to Joshua strengthen your heart for the task ahead.

Success Starts with Following God's Word

To dig a little deeper, list the two specific commands given to Joshua in Joshua 1:8.

❧

❧

According to verse 9, what would happen if Joshua followed God's commands?

What do the following scriptures teach about God's Word?

Psalm 119:11—

Psalm 119:105—

Acts 20:32—

Hebrews 4:12—

1 Peter 1:23—

How can knowing these few facts about the Bible contribute to your success? How do they encourage you to look to the Bible and follow what it says?

> *Either sin will keep you from your Bible or*
> *your Bible will keep you from sin.*

Moving Forward

Read this section in your book again. Write out the steps or actions you were asked to take to fulfill your desire to become a successful woman. Feel free to add any additional items to this list.

As you consider these steps, check the ones you will take today. What difference do you think moving forward on these steps will make in enjoying success God's way as you live out His plan?

2

The Starting Point for Success

This Book of the Law shall not depart from your mouth,
but you shall meditate in it day and night,
that you may observe to do
according to all that is written in it.
For then you will make your way prosperous,
and then you will have good success.

JOSHUA 1:8

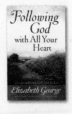 Read chapter 2, "The Starting Point for Success," in *Following God with All Your Heart*. Note any new truths or encouragements that motivate you to tackle what God is asking of you today.

What exciting opportunities are yours today as you seek to follow God? Jot them down and keep them in mind as you work your way through this exciting lesson on trusting God for His will and plan for your life.

Hiding God's Word in Your Heart

Write out Joshua 1:8—from memory if you can.

The Origin of Success

Write down the first five words of Joshua 1:8.

The Bible is God's Word—Look up these verses in your Bible, and note the facts about God's Word.

2 Timothy 3:16—

Hebrews 1:1—

2 Peter 1:20-21—

How should a person who knows the Bible is God's Word approach it? And what difference should it make in his or her life?

The Bible is alive—What do these scriptures reveal about God's Word?

Hebrews 4:12—

1 Peter 1:23—

As you can see, God's Word works on the heart. What difference should these truths make in your life as you read and respond to the Bible?

The Bible is a force—As you read these verses, jot down what you learn about the power and force of God's Word.

Jeremiah 23:29—

Hebrews 4:12—

What should you expect to happen when you read and study the Bible?

The Bible is a defense against temptation—Read Matthew 4:1-11. What words are repeated by Jesus as He was tempted by the devil in:

Verse 4—

Verse 7—

Verse10—

What more do you learn in Ephesians 6:17?

How is God's Word a weapon of offense against temptation and Satan's lies?

The Bible is a guide—We need help as we travel through life. According to the following verses, how does God's Word guide you each step of your way and why should you pay attention to it?

Psalm 19:7—

Psalm 119:105—

Proverbs 6:23—

2 Timothy 3:15—

2 Peter 1:19—

The Power, Influence, and Reward of God's Word

The starting point of success is "this Book of the Law." Scan again the stories in these three sections of chapter 2 about how God's Word makes a difference in the lives of those who read it *and* live by it. What impressed you most?

What message did your heart receive about some of the blessings available to those who desire a greater knowledge and love for the written Word of God?

What changes—or upgrades—can you make in your time in the "Book of the Law" so you will experience greater degrees of the power, influence, and rewards that accompany a passionate pursuit of God's Word?

The Divine Criteria for Success

Read Joshua 1:8 again…in several Bible translations if possible. Write out in your own words God's criteria for success.

Are there any steps or criteria missing in your life that need attention? What needs to be added? Eliminated? Improved?

God's Criteria for Success Lived Out

Who are the women you know (or have known) who live out God's criteria for success? What about them impresses and impacts you most?

What are some of their secrets to success?

Moving Forward

Read this section in your book again. Write out the steps or actions you were asked to take to fulfill your desire to become a successful woman. Feel free to add any additional items to this list.

As you consider these steps, check the ones you will take today. What difference do you think moving forward on these steps will make in enjoying success God's way as you live out His plan?

3

The Road to Success

This Book of the Law shall not depart from your mouth,
but you shall meditate in it day and night,
that you may observe to do according to all that is written in it.
For then you will make your way prosperous,
and then you will have good success.

JOSHUA 1:8

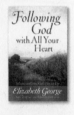 Read chapter 3, "The Road to Success," in *Following God with All Your Heart*. Note any new truths or encouragements that motivate you to tackle what God is asking of you today.

What exciting opportunities are yours today as you seek to follow God? Jot them down and keep them in mind as you work your way through this exciting lesson on trusting God for His will and plan for your life.

Hiding God's Word in Your Heart

Write out Joshua 1:8—from memory if you can.

Success Is Possible for Ordinary People

Look at the definition for success given in the opening paragraph of this chapter. Keep this description in mind as you consider these facts about Joshua.

Joshua was born a slave. Share a few details about your lineage, parents, place of birth, upbringing, education.

Joshua was a student for 50 years before being given great responsibility. Name a few capacities you've served in that qualify as training experiences for future ministry. For instance, did you attend a Christian school or college? What have you volunteered to do at church? Have you served on a committee for a special ministry project or mission?

Joshua fought bouts of fear. Have you? Name a few instances or share situations that are sure to fill you with dread.

Joshua needed ongoing encouragement from God. Share an example or two of how God's Word, a favorite verse, or one of His people encouraged you to keep on keeping on.

Success Is Never Easy

Read again about the many obstacles and challenges Joshua faced on his way to success. What obstacles are making your progress difficult? Maybe something you've never done before or had to handle?

What scripture, example, or encouragement keeps you going when the going gets tough? How can Joshua 1:8 give you the strength to move ahead in the future?

Let's also look at the apostle Paul's life. Look up these scriptures.

2 Timothy 4:7—How did Paul describe his trek on the road to success in ministry and following God with all his heart?

2 Corinthians 11:23-28—What were some of Paul's hurdles and problems along the way to success?

Success Comes from God

Review Joshua's road to success as itemized in Joshua 1:1-9 in your book. Think about your fears and speed bumps. What similarities do you notice between God's personal ministry to Joshua and His role in your situation?

Look again at Joshua 1:8. What can you do today—and every day—to find the guidance and encouragement you need to overcome any and all hindrances to your progress in wholeheartedly following God?

Following in Joshua's Footsteps

Which women in the Bible do you think about when you are up against a barrier or fighting against hopelessness? What about them brings them to mind and encourages you?

"God, Be in My Head"

What does Joshua 1:8 say about God's Word and your mind?

What does Psalm 119:11 reveal about the connection between sin and God's Word in your heart and mind?

As one who has God's Spirit, what does 1 Corinthians 2:16 assure you of?

What is the first thing you are to think on, according to Philippians 4:8? And what truths about God can you think on when you require strength to continue?

Reflecting on Truth

As you discover truths in the Bible and commit them to memory, you can reflect on them anywhere, any time. That's the meditative process. One scholar defined "meditate" in Joshua 1:8 as meaning "recite in an undertone," meaning the meditative pondering and audible practice of orators.[1] In other words, Joshua was to give God's Word constant attention.

What are some of the benefits constant thought and attention to the living Word of God will bring to your daily life...

...when you must perform a duty you'd rather avoid?

...when you experience fear?

...when you are discouraged?

...when you are weak?

...when you are tempted to sin?

Digging into the Truth

What case do these scriptures build for actively studying the Bible?

1 Timothy 4:13—

2 Timothy 2:15—

2 Peter 1:5—

Mary, Jesus' Mother

Read Mary's "Magnificat" in Luke 1:46-55. Write down a few of the many facts about God noted in these verses. What does this outpouring of Old Testament scriptures and God's truths indicate about Mary's heart and mind and her attitude toward God's Word? And what can you do to follow in her steps?

Moving Forward

Read this section in your book again. Write out the steps or actions you were asked to take to fulfill your desire to become a successful woman. Feel free to add any additional items to this list.

As you consider these steps, check the ones you will take today. What difference do you think moving forward on these steps will make in enjoying success God's way as you live out His plan?

4

A Sure Recipe for Success

*This Book of the Law shall not depart from your mouth,
but you shall meditate in it day and night,
that you may observe to do according to all that is written in it.
For then you will make your way prosperous,
and then you will have good success.*

JOSHUA 1:8

Read chapter 4, "A Sure Recipe for Success," in *Following God with All Your Heart*. Note any new truths or encouragements that motivate you to tackle what God is asking of you today.

What exciting opportunities are yours today as you seek to follow God? Jot them down and keep them in mind as you work your way through this exciting lesson on trusting God for His will and plan for your life.

Hiding God's Word in Your Heart

Write out Joshua 1:8—from memory if you can.

Following Instructions

To review, what are the commands given in Joshua 1:8?

1.

2.

3.

What does verse 8 say is the result of following God's instructions?

Obeying God's Word

What do these verses reveal about God's Word and why it should be obeyed?

John 14:15—   Colossians 3:16—

John 15:14—   2 Timothy 3:15-17—

Acts 5:29—   1 Peter 1:22—

Philippians 2:8—

It's much easier to read and memorize Scripture than to obey it, to do it, "to do according to all that is written in it," as Joshua 1:8 tells us. Yet obeying God's Word is an essential step toward enjoying God's brand of success. Are there any areas where you are postponing or delaying obedience to Scripture? Note them now, pray, and then obey. Elisabeth Elliot said, "Delayed obedience is disobedience." That's so true!

Are you sidetracked by something that's interfering with your obedience, like the young man at the beginning of this chapter who was so enthralled with other things that he forgot to follow instructions? Is something keeping you from following God with all your heart? Write it down, pray, and, again, obey!

This section in your book gave a short list of areas for obedience. In a few words, record your obedience level—good, needs improvement, needs radical correction—for each area. Also note action steps you can take today to improve.

Your roles and responsibilities at home—

Your service to others and the church—

Your walk with God—

Your speech—

How Not to Succeed

The Israelites failed to trust God and take Him at His word (see Numbers 14:1-3). They even sought to kill those who encouraged them to follow God (see verses 6-7 and 10). What role does trusting God and taking Him at His word play in becoming a successful woman? Or, put another way, what happens when you disobey God, and what happens when you obey Him (Joshua 1:8)?

Tasting God's Success

In contrast to the failure, defeat, and suffering God's people experienced due to their lack of trust and desire to obey God, how was Joshua successful and blessed? Read the summary in your book and the following verses that highlight each success. Jot down the facts and your thoughts.

Joshua was successful against his enemies (Exodus 17:8-13)—

Joshua was successful in battle (Joshua 3–12)—

Joshua was successful in his assignments (Joshua 13–19)—

Joshua was successful in his personal life (Joshua 19:49)—

Obedience 101

Admission of disobedience and sin clears the way for forgiveness, worship, fellowship, freedom from guilt, and success. What do these verses reveal about the importance of responding in obedience to God's Word?

1 John 1:8-10—

In verses 8 and 10, what is one common excuse regarding sin and disobedience?

According to verse 9, what is our responsibility when we sin? And how are we blessed?

2 Samuel 12:1-14—When David committed a chain of sins, God sent His prophet Nathan to rebuke David. How did God view David's sin in...

verse 9—

verse 10—

What were the consequences (verses 10 and 11)?

Think about it. Even though David confessed his sin (verse 13), he still reaped the consequences, just as Nathan prophesied. Chapters 13–20 of 1 Samuel record David's heartache, family issues, and the effects of his failure to obey God. Although he was forgiven and once again enjoyed fellowship with God, he didn't enjoy the level of success he'd known during his decades of heartfelt obedience, of following God with all his heart.

Now look at Nehemiah 9:1-3. How did these Israelites approach the Law of God and respond to His Word? Also note what impresses you most. In other words, what can you incorporate into your heart and your Bible-reading time now?

Moving Forward

Read this section in your book again. Write out the steps or actions you were asked to take to fulfill your desire to become a successful woman. Feel free to add any additional items to this list.

As you consider these steps, check the ones you will take today. What difference do you think moving forward on these steps will make in enjoying success God's way as you live out His plan?

5

Focusing for Greatness

Have I not commanded you?
Be strong and of good courage;
do not be afraid, nor be dismayed,
for the LORD your God is with you wherever you go.

JOSHUA 1:9

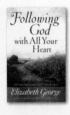

Read chapter 5, "Focusing for Greatness," in *Following God with All Your Heart*. Note any new truths or encouragements that motivate you to tackle what God is asking of you today.

What exciting opportunities are yours today as you seek to follow God? Jot them down and keep them in mind as you work your way through this exciting lesson on trusting God for His will and plan for your life.

Hiding God's Word in Your Heart

Memorize Joshua 1:9. Write down how it appears in your favorite version of the Bible. You may want to look at a few other translations and note any words that differ to help you better understand the meaning of this powerful verse. What part of this verse really stands out and speaks to your heart today?

Power Can Come in Small Packages

Write out the first sentence in Joshua 1:9.

What commands and instructions has God already given Joshua in...

verse 2—

verse 6—

verse 7 (list them both)—

verse 8 (list all three)—

verse 9 (list all four)—

What is God telling you to do today that you are uncertain about?

What first step can you take to begin the "Grand Canyon effect" so you can experience the power that comes with obedience to God's commands and guidance?

How does Proverbs 3:5 help you?

How is faith and trust in God defined in Hebrews 11:1?

The Road to Success

The book gives an overview of what makes a woman successful in

God's eyes. As you read again about the efforts involved, jot down
a brief evaluation of your endeavors on each point...and then set
a goal for improvement.

❧ She diligently grows in her knowledge of God and
His Word.

❧ She faithfully hides God's Word in her heart.

❧ She carefully thinks on God's Word at all times and
in every situation.

❧ She thoroughly carries out God's Word through
obedience.

Following God...No Matter What

Joseph—With your Bible in hand, look at these scriptures and follow
Joseph's path to greatness as he followed God with all his heart.
Take notes along the way.

Genesis 37:3-4—

Genesis 37:18-20,27—

Genesis 39:1-2—

Genesis 39:20-21—

Genesis 41:39-44—

Daniel—Read about Daniel's path to greatness and take notes along the way.

Daniel 1:1-4,6—

Daniel 1:8-9—

Daniel 1:17-20—

Daniel 2:48—

Esther—Esther has been referred to by many as "the queen of courage." Chart her path to greatness, jotting down your observations as you read the following scriptures:

Esther 2:5-7—

Esther 2:2-4,8-9—

Esther 2:16-17—

Ruth—Ruth's success and greatness were forged out of sorrow and heartache. As you read in your Bible, make notes on her life and God's goodness.

Ruth 1:1-5—

Ruth 1:6-8,14-16,22—

Ruth 4:13,17—

Mary, the mother of Jesus—She is the most well-known woman ever to live, yet her road had humble beginnings. Write out what you learn about her heart and her path to greatness in the following verses:

Luke 1:26-31—

Luke 1:38—

Luke 1:48-49—

List some of the common denominators in these people's lives that caused them to rise above their difficult circumstances.

Moving Forward

Read this section in your book again. Write out the steps or actions you were asked to take to fulfill your desire to become a courageous woman. Feel free to add any additional items to this list.

As you consider these steps, check the ones you will take today. What difference do you think moving forward on these steps will make in strengthening your courage as you live out God's plan?

6

Facing the Impossible

Have I not commanded you?
Be strong and of good courage;
do not be afraid, nor be dismayed,
for the LORD your God is with you wherever you go.

JOSHUA 1:9

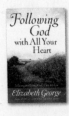 Read chapter 6, "Facing the Impossible," in *Following God with All Your Heart*. Note any new truths or encouragements that motivate you to tackle what God is asking of you today.

What exciting opportunities are yours today as you seek to follow God? Jot them down and keep them in mind as you work your way through this exciting lesson on trusting God for His will and plan for your life.

Hiding God's Word in Your Heart

Write out Joshua 1:9—from memory if you can.

Seven Habits for Gaining Strength and Courage

Think through the past few days and pinpoint any problems that popped up. What was your first response generally? Exasperation? Fear? Irritation? Others?

Now read Joshua 1:9 again in your favorite version of the Bible. What are God's commands?

❧

❧

❧

❧

1. *Know God's character*—Read Numbers 14:1-9. What do you learn about the character of the Israelites when they ran up against a problem? Briefly describe their behavior and response.

   What do you learn in verse 9 about the character of God?

How is hesitation and frustration viewed by God?

What is said about fear, and upon what is it based?

Now read 2 Corinthians 2:14. What truth do you learn about God's character? And, as you were asked in the book, do you believe this?

How does the truth about God's character encourage you to be more courageous as you face your problems?

2. *Embrace God's plan for you*—When you acknowledge and embrace God's roles, responsibilities, duties, and job assignments for you and move forward in obedience, what does Joshua 1:8 promise?

What does Joshua 1:9 promise as you face the impossible?

What are some of your responsibilities? Here's a partial list of possibilities to start you off:

X being a student   ? meeting a deadline
✓ working at a job   X heading up a ministry
X caring for your husband X assisting elderly parents
X raising your children   ___
✓ *paying someone's debts* ___

As you look at your list, how do you gain strength based on God's character and promises?

What is your favorite verse for courage in the Bible, and why?

3. *Be around older Christian women*—What does Titus 2:3-5 say about the "older women" in the church? And the "younger women"?

Think about a mature woman of faith you admire. What qualities of hers do you desire to develop and why?

4. *Don't listen to the world*—What does Romans 12:2 say about your attitude and approach to the world?

According to Ephesians 2:1-3, what was your former relationship with the world and what is it to be now as a believer in Christ?

And what about 1 John 2:15-16?

5. *Recite "Someone has to…" and fill in the blank*—Look at your responsibilities. Is there anything you're putting off or failing to do that falls on your shoulders? As you recite "Someone has to…" and fill in the blank, how does realizing the truth of this statement bolster you with the strength and resolve to take the task on, to wade into the waters and do what must be done? Note a step or two you can take now.

6. *Study God's Word*—You've probably heard the expression "Put on your thinking cap." How is studying God's Word like putting on a fresh thinking cap? How does His Word alter your thinking and perspective regarding your situation, challenges, and problems?

7. *Remember the women at the cross.* Briefly scan Mark 15:39–16:1-11. What do you learn about these women of courage in…

Mark 15:39-40—

Mark 15:46-47—

Mark 16:1-3—

How were these women blessed and rewarded, as recorded in Matthew 28:9?

What is your present problem, and how will remembering the women at the cross help you face it and see it through?

Moving Forward

Read this section in your book again. Write out the steps or actions you were asked to take to fulfill your desire to become a courageous woman. Feel free to add any additional items to this list.

As you consider these steps, check the ones you will take today. What difference do you think moving forward on these steps will make in strengthening your courage as you live out God's plan?

7

Fighting Your Fears

Have I not commanded you?
Be strong and of good courage;
do not be afraid, nor be dismayed,
for the LORD *your God is with you wherever you go.*

JOSHUA 1:9

Read chapter 7, "Fighting Your Fears," in *Following God with All Your Heart*. Note any new truths or encouragements that motivate you to tackle what God is asking of you today.

What exciting opportunities are yours today as you seek to follow God? Jot them down and keep them in mind as you work your way through this exciting lesson on trusting God for His will and plan for your life.

Hiding God's Word in Your Heart

Write out Joshua 1:9—from memory if you can.

Count on God's Promise

What does Joshua 1:9 reveal about one of God's attributes—His omnipresence...His ever-presence?

What does 2 Peter 1:4 tell you about God's promises?

Every Divine promise is built upon four pillars:

God's holiness, *which will not suffer Him to deceive;*

His goodness, *which will not suffer Him to forget;*

His truth, *which will not suffer Him to change; and*

His power, *which makes Him able to accomplish!* [1]

How does the promise in Joshua 1:9 encourage you as you stand on the threshold of facing your giants and fighting your fears today?

Pay Attention to the Don'ts

Sometimes a negative speaks as loudly as a positive. What two bits of negative instruction—two *don'ts*—did God give to Joshua in Joshua 1:9? Be sure to look up each one in a dictionary.

❧ don't be _____

❧ don't be _____

How are these emotions opposites to the strength and courage God calls us to? And how do they stand in the way of doing God's will and following Him with all your heart?

Look once again at the promises made to Joshua. Note how they would strengthen and encourage him.

Joshua 1:3—

verse 5—

verse 9—

Make it a point to remember your heavenly Father—His character and attributes—and review His promises when you face fear and discouragement. Name two of God's exceedingly great and precious promises that especially support you in difficult and trying times.

❧

❧

Strength in the Midst of Fear

Can you think of any real-life heroes? Briefly share what makes them heroes in your eyes.

How do you see strength in Joshua exhibited, as reported in Joshua 1:10-11?

What's in Front of You?

What is God expecting you to do right now? And how are you responding and why?

When I know someone is going through a tough challenge I always ask, "What verse are you using to help get you through?" Joshua 1:9 is one of my "helping" verses. What about you? How does Joshua 1:9 fortify you to tackle your Number One challenge today?

Facing Your Giants

The list of fearful, distressing challenges could indeed go on and on. Glance through this partial list of several types of problems and challenges. Which one or ones are you facing today? Add to the list the other issues you're dealing with.

___ physical problems   ___ time problems

___ marriage and family problems   ___ financial problems

___ job or school problems   ___ other issues

What principles, instructions, and promises have you discovered in Joshua 1:9 that you can apply as you face your giants?

Victory Is Yours!

Victory is what Joshua 1:9 is all about. Think once again about:

God's will—What is He asking of you, commanding you to do, expecting of you?

God's presence—How does the fact and truth of God being with you through all things and at all times strengthen and encourage you to move forward to victory?

What did the psalmist declare in:

Psalm 18:1—

Psalm 27:1—

Psalm 46:1—

Psalm 68:35—

Psalm 73:26—

Psalm 84:5 and 7—

Psalm 138:3—

How are you strengthened by the knowledge of God's love, power, presence, and strength as you deal with your daily opportunities to trust Him?

Look again at the final words in Psalm 68:35. How will you do the same today?

Moving Forward

Read this section in your book again. Write out the steps or actions you were asked to take to fulfill your desire to become a courageous woman. Feel free to add any additional items to this list.

As you consider these steps, check the ones you will take today. What difference do you think moving forward on these steps will make in strengthening your courage as you live out God's plan?

8

Counting On the Presence of God

Have I not commanded you?
Be strong and of good courage;
do not be afraid, nor be dismayed,
for the LORD your God is with you wherever you go.

JOSHUA 1:9

Read chapter 8, "Counting On the Presence of God," in *Following God with All Your Heart*. Note any new truths or encouragements that motivate you to tackle what God is asking of you today.

What exciting opportunities are yours today as you seek to follow God? Jot them down and keep them in mind as you work your way through this exciting lesson on trusting God for His will and plan for your life.

Hiding God's Word in Your Heart
Write out Joshua 1:9—from memory if you can.

The God Who Is There
Read Psalm 139:7-12 and note what you learn about God—the God who is there—from...

verses 7-8—

verses 9-10—

verses 11-12—

The God Who Is Not Silent
The book of Joshua has much to say about God's active presence. Look at these evidences of His involvement in leading and encouraging Joshua each step of the way as Joshua followed after God with all his heart. How do you see God also making Himself known...

...to Rahab and the people of Jericho (Joshua 2:8-13)—

...to the Israelites (Joshua 3:14-17)—

...to Joshua, the Israelites, and the people of Jericho (Joshua 6:20-21)—

...to Joshua, the Israelites, and God's enemies (Joshua 10:8-11)—

...to Joshua, the Israelites, and God's enemies (Joshua 10:12-13)—

...to Joshua (Joshua 11:6)—

What About God's Presence in Your Life?

Do you ever wonder about or doubt God's presence in your life? Does the thought of Him being constantly with you frighten you? Do you wonder how He might make His presence known? Share the thoughts you have most often about God's presence.

God's presence is not limited—What does John 4:20-24 reveal about the presence of God?

God's presence is spiritual—Read John 14:16-17, 1 Corinthians 6:19, and 2 Corinthians 6:16. In your own words, what truth do these verses teach about God's presence in believers?

God's presence is real—David, the psalmist who wrote Psalm 23, knew God's presence was real and found peace, strength, comfort, and courage in that knowledge. Note the truths about God's presence in each verse of Psalm 23...even though He is not seen.

Verse 1—

Verse 2—

Verse 3—

Verse 4—

Verse 5—

Verse 6—

God's presence is a good thing—How did the psalmist view God's presence in Psalm 46:1, and what effect did it have on him in verses 2 and 3?

How did David count on God's presence, as noted in Psalm 138:7?

Sin hinders our relationship with God. That's fact. God never moves away from us, but we move away from Him. What guidance, answers, and results do we find to restore our closeness to God in these scriptures?

Psalm 32:1-5—

Psalm 38:17-18—

Psalm 51:1-3,8,12, and 17—

1 John 1:8—

1 John 1:9—

1 John 1:10—

God's presence is a comfort—Read Psalm 34:17-19. What comfort do you find here?

What do you learn about the ministry of the indwelling Holy Spirit from John 14:16?

How is God referred to in 2 Corinthians 1:3, and how does He minister to you?

God's presence is empowering—Following God with all your heart requires strength, courage, and power. What is the truth found in...

Psalm 27:1—

Psalm 46:1—

Psalm 68:35—

Psalm 73:26—

Psalm 138:3—

Philippians 4:13—

Moving Forward

Read this section in your book again. Write out the steps or actions you were asked to take to fulfill your desire to become a courageous woman. Feel free to add any additional items to this list.

As you consider these steps, check the ones you will take today. What difference do you think moving forward on these steps will make in strengthening your courage as you live out God's plan?

9

Living Above the Norm

Do not be conformed to this world,
but be transformed by the renewing of your mind,
that you may prove what is that good and
acceptable and perfect will of God.

ROMANS 12:2

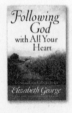

Read chapter 9, "Living Above the Norm," in _Following_
God with All Your Heart. Note any new truths or encouragements that motivate you to tackle what God is asking
of you today.

What exciting opportunities are yours today as you seek to follow
God? Jot them down and keep them in mind as you work your way
through this exciting lesson on trusting God for His will and plan
for your life.

Hiding God's Word in Your Heart

Memorize Romans 12:2. Write down how it appears in your favorite version of the Bible. You may want to look at a few other translations and note any words that differ to help you better understand the meaning of this powerful verse. What part of this verse really stands out and speaks to your heart today?

The Fork in the Road

At what "fork in the road" does life find you today? Write out your situation and any decisions you must make to follow God with all your heart.

How does God's command to "not be conformed to this world" assist in decisions you'll be making now or in the near future?

What helps you discern God's will from the world's ways as revealed in these scriptures?

Psalm 23:3—

Psalm 119:105—

Proverbs 4:27—

Matthew 7:13-14—

Be on Your Guard

What do these verses teach about vigilance in the Christian life?

Ephesians 4:27—

Ephesians 6:11—

1 Peter 1:13—

1 Peter 1:14—

1 Peter 5:8—

1 John 4:1—

Look at 1 Peter 5:8 again. Who is a believer's ultimate enemy, and what is his goal?

Ordinary or Extraordinary?

What are some necessary elements in your quest to live an extraordinary life, as shown in 1 Thessalonians 5:16-22?

Verse 16—

Verse 17—

Verse 18—

Verse 19—

Verse 20—

Verse 21—

Verse 22—

Are any of these missing from your daily practices? Check them now and determine to make changes, to follow God's instructions!

God's Roll Call of Exceptional Women

Briefly scan the following scriptures and their descriptions of several of God's exceptional women. Jot down one or two qualities about each of these women who lived above the norm, who stood out as women who loved and followed God.

Ruth (Ruth 1–2)—

The Proverbs 31 woman (Proverbs 31:10-31)—

Mary, Jesus' mother (Luke 1:26-56)—

Elizabeth (Luke 1:5-7,39-45)—

Sarah (1 Peter 3:1-6; Hebrews 11:11)—

Now note one or two of their qualities that you desire to strengthen in your life or make your own.

Becoming an Exceptional Woman

How would you evaluate yourself with respect to these steps to becoming an exceptional woman?

☐ Good   ☐ Needs Attention

If you checked "Needs Attention," what can you do to...

...guard your intake?

...select your friends more carefully?

...spend your time on what really matters?

...watch what you wear?

Moving Forward

Read this section in your book again. Write out the steps or actions you were asked to take to fulfill your desire to become an exceptional woman. Feel free to add any additional items to this list.

As you consider these steps, check the ones you will take today. What difference do you think moving forward on these steps will make in living out God's plan in an exceptional manner?

10

Making a Difference

Do not be conformed to this world,
but be transformed by the renewing of your mind,
that you may prove what is that good and
acceptable and perfect will of God.

ROMANS 12:2

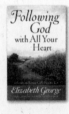 Read chapter 10, "Making a Difference," in *Following God with All Your Heart*. Note any new truths or encouragements that motivate you to tackle what God is asking of you today.

What exciting opportunities are yours today as you seek to follow God? Jot them down and keep them in mind as you work your way through this exciting lesson on trusting God for His will and plan for your life.

Hiding God's Word in Your Heart

Write out Romans 12:2—from memory if you can.

A Remarkable Change

How do these verses describe the transformation that takes place in believers?

Ezekiel 36:25-27—

John 3:3—

Romans 6:4—

2 Corinthians 5:17—

Galatians 2:20—

Ephesians 4:21-24—

1 John 3:2—

Don't forget to pause and give thanks to God for His Son and all He accomplished for you.

Living in the World

Read these verses and comment on why we struggle in this world.

John 7:7—

John 15:18-19—

1 Corinthians 1:18—

1 John 5:19—

2 John 7—

In your own words, describe how you are to live in the world using the following guidelines:

By being salt (Matthew 5:13)—

By being light (Matthew 5:14)—

By making a difference as:

an ambassador (2 Corinthians 5:20)—

a preacher of the gospel (Romans 10:14-15)—

Let Transformation Begin!

Renewing your mind involves the following areas.

Your speech—What do these verses say about your speech?

Proverbs 10:11—

Proverbs 10:20—

Matthew 12:34—

Ephesians 4:15—

Ephesians 4:25—

Ephesians 4:29—

Ephesians 4:31—

Colossians 3:8—

James 5:12—

Take a moment to note what needs improvement in your life.

Your habits—What do these verses say about your habits...or lack of them?

Proverbs 12:24—

Proverbs 20:4—

Proverbs 26:14—

Proverbs 26:15—

Colossians 3:23—

As you can tell, there's nothing extraordinary about the negatives in these scriptures. Did you find any habits that require radical treatment and attention from you so you can truly follow God with all your heart and make a difference? Note them here, put them on your prayer list, ask for God's help, and make the necessary changes.

Your attitudes—What should you put off or put away according to...

Ephesians 4:22?

How is this to be accomplished (verse 23)?

What should you put on (verse 24)?

How does this new man live (verse 24)?

Make a to-do list of what you will put off and put on as soon as possible.

Remolding Your Mind

Once again, list the two steps involved in remolding your mind according to Romans 12:2, and decide what you're going to do about these two commands from God.

Step 1—

Step 2—

Moving Forward

Read this section in your book again. Write out the steps or actions you were asked to take to fulfill your desire to become an exceptional woman. Feel free to add any additional items to this list.

As you consider these steps, check the ones you will take today. What difference do you think moving forward on these steps will make in living out God's plan in an exceptional manner?

11

Renewing Your Mind

Do not be conformed to this world,
but be transformed by the renewing of your mind,
that you may prove what is that good and
acceptable and perfect will of God.

ROMANS 12:2

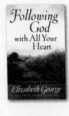 Read chapter 11, "Renewing Your Mind," in *Following God with All Your Heart*. Note any new truths or encouragements that motivate you to tackle what God is asking of you today.

What exciting opportunities are yours today as you seek to follow God? Jot them down and keep them in mind as you work your way through this exciting lesson on trusting God for His will and plan for your life.

Hiding God's Word in Your Heart

Write out Romans 12:2—from memory if you can.

Reflecting the Image of Christ

Your ultimate goal as a Christian is to be like Christ now and in the future. How do the following verses describe this reality?

2 Corinthians 3:18—

Philippians 3:12—

Philippians 3:14—

1 John 3:1-3—

As you reflect on these instructions and truths, what can you do to promote that reality in your life?

Changing Your Thinking Patterns

When someone becomes a Christian, God gives him or her a completely new nature and utterly new spiritual and mental capacities. As a believer, what do the following verses say you have?

1 Corinthians 2:12—

1 Corinthians 2:16—

Even with a new spiritual capacity, you still need to focus your thoughts on godly pursuits. List the limitations set on your thoughts, according to Philippians 4:8:

1.   5.

2.   6.

3.   7.

4.   8.

How will adhering to this guidance help change your thinking patterns?

Are there any restrictions you need to make in your life as you consider Philippians 4:8?

How can the following spiritual disciplines (and your decisions regarding them) assist you in changing your thinking patterns as you follow God with all your heart?

Get alone with God (When?)—

Get into the Book (What will you read today?)—

Get the right perspective on prayer (Again, when?)—

Get the Book in you (What will you memorize?)—

Get your growth down on paper (Why not write one summary
sentence a day?)—

Get together with God's people (What about this week?)—

Get a few close friends (Why not schedule time with committed
Christians this week?)—

Get your heart to talk (Why not develop an opening question to
get godly conversation started?)—

Revealing the Real You

What changes need to occur so you will be further transformed and
become more like Christ?

Moving Forward

Read this section in your book again. Write out the steps or actions you were asked to take to fulfill your desire to become an exceptional woman. Feel free to add any additional items to this list.

As you consider these steps, check the ones you will take today. What difference do you think moving forward on these steps will make in living out God's plan in an exceptional manner?

12

Living God's Will

Do not be conformed to this world,
but be transformed by the renewing of your mind,
that you may prove what is that good and
acceptable and perfect will of God.

ROMANS 12:2

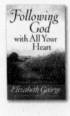 Read chapter 12, "Living God's Will," in *Following God with All Your Heart*. Note any new truths or encouragements that motivate you to tackle what God is asking of you today.

What exciting opportunities are yours today as you seek to follow God? Jot them down and keep them in mind as you work your way through this exciting lesson on trusting God for His will and plan for your life.

Hiding God's Word in Your Heart

Write out Romans 12:2—from memory if you can.

The Amazing Will of God

All of God's Word contains God's will. His will has two aspects. There is the will of God by which He *decrees* what comes to pass. This aspect will *always* be accomplished. What does Romans 8:29-30 say about God's will?

There is also the side of God's will that *desires* that His people obey His prohibitions and His affirmations. Theologians call this God's *permissive* will. This means there is an opportunity for obedience. As you read these verses in your Bible, note some of the aspects of this side of God's will and your role and responsibilities.

Romans 12:2—

1 Thessalonians 5:18—

1 Peter 2:13-15—

1 Peter 3:17—

Hebrews 10:36—

God's will is good—It couldn't be otherwise because God is good. What did God say about Himself when Moses asked to see His glory (Exodus 33:19)?

How did God express His goodness to Israel in Jeremiah 29:11?

How do you respond to Jeremiah 29:11 as it applies to you today?

God's will is acceptable—When we follow God with all our hearts and do His will, it pleases Him. We please God by doing His will. What did God the Father say at His Son's baptism (Matthew 3:17)?

God's will is perfect—Look up a definition of "perfect," and then describe how God's will is perfect.

Understanding God's Will

God's will begins with renewing your mind—Reread this section and then put its meaning in your own words.

God's will gives meaning to your life—God gave meaning to the prophet Jeremiah's life in Jeremiah 1:5. Read Ephesians 1:11-14 and describe how God gives meaning to your life too.

God's will is unique to you—You are one of a kind. You were saved as an individual, and you were specially created for God's service. Read 1 Corinthians 12:4-11, and then describe your unique giftedness. (Pay close attention to verses 7 and 11.)

God's will requires patience—What does 2 Peter 3:8 say about God's view of time?

What does Galatians 4:4 say about the coming of Jesus Christ?

What does 2 Peter 3:9 say about God's patience toward the lost?

God's timing on all things is perfect. He is patient with you, so how should you view the working out of God's will in your life?

God's will requires obedience—Read Acts 16:6-10 and briefly describe how Paul's missionary team responded to God's unfolding will... and the result.

Finding God's Will

Living in God's will makes us exceptional women. And God wants us to find and know His will even more than we want to! Here's how you can discover and discern it.

Begin with God's Word—God's Word is God's will, so it's the starting point. How faithful have you been in reading and studying the Bible, and what steps can you take to improve in this important endeavor?

Don't forget to pray!—Before you need to make another decision, sit down and create (or photocopy) the following chart that highlights four crucial considerations. Ask and answer these questions for each decision, and then, with your heart and motives exposed and your convictions uncovered, pray for God's leading.

1. Why would I do this?
2. Why would I not do this?
3. Why should I do this?
4. Why should I not do this?

Share an instance of how this exercise worked for you this week.

Safeguard by asking for advice—List several people you can go to for advice on difficult issues.

❧

❧

❧

If you can't think of anyone, ask God to provide this important resource in your life.

Factor in your personal life—Think about your present situation, season of life, job, family responsibilities, and so forth. Don't forget to lay each decision you have to make next to this picture of your personal life. How will factoring in your life season help guide you in decision making and temper the desires of your heart?

Do God's Will

List any decision(s) you are presently facing. Have you followed the steps listed under the section entitled "Finding God's Will"? If not, do so at your first opportunity.

> *To know God's will is man's greatest treasure;*
>
> *to do His will is life's greatest privilege.*[1]

Waiting for God's Will to Unfold

Look up the following scriptures and note the many things you *know* are God's will. Share your progress in these areas...and continue to follow after God with all your heart, soul, strength, and mind!

2 Peter 3:9—

Romans 8:29—

Ephesians 5:22-33—

Deuteronomy 6:5 and 7—

1 Thessalonians 4:4-5—

Acts 1:8—

Moving Forward

Read this section in your book again. Write out the steps or actions you were asked to take to fulfill your desire to become an exceptional woman. Feel free to add any additional items to this list.

As you consider these steps, check the ones you will take today. What difference do you think moving forward on these steps will make in living out God's plan in an exceptional manner?

13

Laying a Foundation of Humility

All of you be submissive to one another,
and be clothed with humility, for
"God resists the proud, but gives grace to the humble."
Therefore humble yourselves under the mighty hand of God,
that He may exalt you in due time.

1 PETER 5:5-6

 Read chapter 13, "Laying a Foundation of Humility," in *Following God with All Your Heart*. Note any new truths or encouragements that motivate you to tackle what God is asking of you today.

What exciting opportunities are yours today as you seek to follow God? Jot them down and keep them in mind as you work your way through this exciting lesson on trusting God for His will and plan for your life.

Hiding God's Word in Your Heart

Memorize 1 Peter 5:5-6. Write down how it appears in your favorite version of the Bible. You may want to look at a few other translations and note any words that differ to help you better understand the meaning of this powerful verse. What part of this verse really stands out and speaks to your heart today?

Discovering a New Kind of Power

The apostle Peter begins chapter 5 of this epistle by admonishing the church's leadership to feed and lead those under their care (1 Peter 5:1-2). They were not to lord it over the people but to be role models (verse 3). Peter then charged the people to honor and respect their church leaders.

Who are the first group of people he addresses (verse 5)?

Who are the second group of people, and what were they advised to do...and to what extent?

What was Peter's additional request of the people regarding their "clothing"?

What truths about God does Peter share in verse 5?

ʔ▸

ʔ▸

How do these truths make humble submission to everybody easier?

Humility—God's Great Virtue

Describe Jesus' attitude and actions while on earth, as shown in the following verses.

Matthew 11:29—

John 13:3-5—

Philippians 2:8 (note Jesus' four acts of humility)—

❧

❧

❧

❧

Now read Philippians 2:3 and 4. How is it similar to 1 Peter 5:5 in instructing you in the way you should deal with others?

Looking at God's Plan for You

Peter had come a long way on his journey toward humility. In the following verses note some of his brash actions as a younger man that highlight how far he traveled and what helped him on the road to humility.

Matthew 16:22-23—

John 18:10-11—

Matthew 26:69-70—

Matthew 26:71-72—

Matthew 26:73-75—

Have you been brash in the past? What instances can you recall, and what has helped you become a more humble woman today? (Write down at least one incident.)

Three Actions that Nurture Humility

You can always look to God for help with humility and grace to empower you to defer to others and rank yourself beneath them.

1. *Choose to defer to others*—Write out a dictionary definition of "defer."

Read Luke 2:41-52 and describe Jesus' actions.

Think of someone God is asking you to be humble with. How will Jesus' example help you defer to that person?

2. *Choose to submit yourself*—You read several definitions for "submission" and "submissive" in your book. Now write out a dictionary definition for "submission."

How does Dr. Charles Ryrie's description of submission help you apply humility in your life?

3. *Choose to rank yourself under others*—In the book of 1 Peter there are numerous categories or areas for submission and deference mentioned. For instance, in 1 Peter 5:5, what categories are addressed?

And in 1 Peter 2:13?

And in verse 14?

And in verse 18?

Humility is a choice. What did you learn from the three actions covered in this section about humility and the need for God's grace?

Is there an area where you need to make a choice to follow God and humbly submit to another? If so, what are you going to do about it?

A Word to the Wise

We are to be submissive to one another, but the Bible also specifically asks married women to show this attitude of respect to their husbands. Whether you're married or not, write out what is said to wives in the following verses.

1 Corinthians 11:3—

Ephesians 5:22—

Ephesians 5:24—

Colossians 3:18—

Titus 2:5—

1 Peter 3:1—

1 Peter 3:5-6—

If you are married, is there an area where you need to make a choice to follow God by humbly submitting to your husband? If so, what are you going to do about it? If you aren't married, share your thoughts about submission gleaned from this study.

Moving Forward

Read this section in your book again. Write out the steps or actions you were asked to take to fulfill your desire to become a humble woman. Feel free to add any additional items to this list.

As you consider these steps, check the ones you will take today. What difference do you think moving forward on these steps will make in living out God's plan in a humble manner?

14

Putting On a Heart of Humility

All of you be submissive to one another,
and be clothed with humility, for
"God resists the proud, but gives grace to the humble."
Therefore humble yourselves under the mighty hand of God,
that He may exalt you in due time.

1 Peter 5:5-6

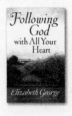

Read chapter 14, "Putting On a Heart of Humility," in *Following God with All Your Heart*. Note any new truths or encouragements that motivate you to tackle what God is asking of you today.

What exciting opportunities are yours today as you seek to follow God? Jot them down and keep them in mind as you work your way through this exciting lesson on trusting God for His will and plan for your life.

Hiding God's Word in Your Heart

Write out 1 Peter 5:5-6—from memory if you can.

Submission, the Beginnings of Humility

Read again about my encounter with the "First Lady." Was her humility a result of her submissive spirit? Or was her submissive heart created by her humility? What do you think?

Describe why submission is basic to the foundation...

...of church relationships

...of unity

...of peace

...of progress

A Personal Story

Make a list of who and what you are to submit to. You may want to refer back to 1 Peter and the partial list in the previous lesson.

Offer a brief statement of your actions—and attitudes—toward the people on your list. Do you need to make any changes? And how can you improve on this attitude that is foundational in all relationships?

The Scope of Humility

In 1 Peter 5:5, God gives two commands. List them here:

❧

❧

As you look at your answers, what do you learn regarding the scope of submission and humility?

What reason does Peter give for following these commands?

To comply with God's command to be submissive and serve one another, what clothing does Peter say you need to put on because you want to wholeheartedly follow God?

Humility is an attitude toward others—The apostle Paul was a giant of the Christian faith in the early church and the writer of 13 books of the New Testament. And yet he possessed a submissive spirit. Read how "the apostle of the gentiles" responded to the elders during his final visit to Jerusalem (Acts 21:19-26). What was the elders' request (verses 23-24)?

How did Paul respond (verse 26)?

Humility is a garment to be worn—Read these verses in your Bible and note what clothing you are to put on.

Colossians 3:12—

Colossians 3:14—

1 Timothy 3:9-10—

1 Peter 3:4—

1 Peter 5:5—

Read about Jesus' humble service in John 13:1-5. With His example in mind, pinpoint someone in your life for whom you must "gird"

Putting On a Heart of Humility ❧ 99

yourself with the garment of humility so you can serve him or her. Be specific in what actions you will take.

Humility is a denial of self—Paul was the architect of much of our understanding of Christian doctrine and teachings. And he practiced what he preached. How did he remind the Ephesian leaders of his selfless attitude during his ministry (Acts 20:31,33-35)?

What was their response to his actions toward them (verses 37-38)?

Since humility is a denial of self and takes place in the heart and mind, think of several actions you can take this week that will demonstrate your willingness to deny yourself and selflessly serve others. Be specific.

Humility is active cooperation—Think of a recent instance when your act of submission was present but your humility was not. What do you need to do? Ask forgiveness? Acknowledge the lesson you've learned? Be on guard in the future? Make sure you put on humility each morning? Seek a better understanding of humility? Humble yourself under the mighty hand of God, as 1 Peter 5:6 suggests? Note what you're going to do, why you need to do it, and when. Pray about your need for God's grace and humility and follow through.

Moving Forward

Read this section in your book again. Write out the steps or actions you were asked to take to fulfill your desire to become a humble woman. Feel free to add any additional items to this list.

As you consider these steps, check the ones you will take today. What difference do you think moving forward on these steps will make in living out God's plan in a humble manner?

15

Seeing Humility in $\mathcal{A}$*ction*

All of you be submissive to one another,
and be clothed with humility, for
"God resists the proud, but gives grace to the humble."
Therefore humble yourselves under the mighty hand of God,
that He may exalt you in due time.

1 Peter 5:5-6

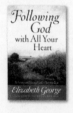

Read chapter 15, "Seeing Humility in Action," in *Following God with All Your Heart*. Note any new truths or encouragements that motivate you to tackle what God is asking of you today.

What exciting opportunities are yours today as you seek to follow God? Jot them down and keep them in mind as you work your way through this exciting lesson on trusting God for His will and plan for your life.

Hiding God's Word in Your Heart

Write out 1 Peter 5:5-6—from memory if you can.

Expressions of Humility

The attitude of humility has "footprints." Track its origins and its destination in the following examples and expressions.

Humility Follows in Jesus' Footsteps

Read Philippians 2:6-8 and state why Jesus' stay on earth provides the greatest example of humility. Also note the evidences and actions of the Lord's humility in each verse listed.

Verse 6—

Verse 7—

Verse 8—

Now look at verse 5. What command is given for nurturing humility?

Look up 1 Peter 2:21-23. How are you to act and follow Jesus' example when you're persecuted or treated unjustly?

What three responses in verses 21-23 involve the mouth?

What is the message to you?

Read Hebrews 12:1-2. What instructions does verse 1 give you about following God with all your heart for life?

According to verse 2, how can you make this a reality and sustain it?

Humility Develops a Servant's Heart

Look up the following verses. What term does your favorite version of the Bible use for Paul's description of himself?

Romans 1:1—

Philippians 1:1—

Titus 1:1—

As a servant of Christ, Paul asked others to follow his example. Write out what he asked of his readers.

1 Corinthians 11:1—

Philippians 3:17—

Philippians 4:9—

Describe how these two disciples of Paul followed his example of humble service and responded with instant obedience.

Timothy (Philippians 2:19-23)—

Epaphroditus (Philippians 2:25-30)—

Jesus, Paul, and these two men followed God with all their hearts. They also show us the way to humble service and how to walk that path. As you consider their examples, what changes will you put in place in your life? And what truths will you take away for further spiritual growth?

Humility Possesses a Helpful Spirit

Drawing on your own experiences, comment on these opposites of humility. Are you or have you been guilty of any of these actions? If yes, what steps will you take to turn your negatives into positive humility?

The "last word" woman—

The "know-it-all" woman—

The "I can top your day" woman—

The "question everything" woman—

The "reluctant" woman—

After reading this chapter and looking at the lives of Jesus and others, how can you nurture humility as you follow God unconditionally? What actions and attitudes come to mind?

Moving Forward

Read this section in your book again. Write out the steps or actions you were asked to take to fulfill your desire to become a humble woman. Feel free to add any additional items to this list.

As you consider these steps, check the ones you will take today. What difference do you think moving forward on these steps will make in living out God's plan in a humble manner?

16

Walking the Less-Traveled Road of Humility

All of you be submissive to one another,
and be clothed with humility, for
"God resists the proud, but gives grace to the humble."
Therefore humble yourselves under the mighty hand of God,
that He may exalt you in due time.

1 PETER 5:5-6

Read chapter 16, "Walking the Less-Traveled Road of Humility," in *Following God with All Your Heart*. Note any new truths or encouragements that motivate you to tackle what God is asking of you today.

What exciting opportunities are yours today as you seek to follow God? Jot them down and keep them in mind as you work your way through this exciting lesson on trusting God for His will and plan for your life.

Hiding God's Word in Your Heart

Write out 1 Peter 5:5-6—from memory if you can.

Knowing More About God Promotes Humility

Four facts about God provide direction in your quest for a life of humility.

Fact #1: God resists the proud—Ezekiel 28 begins with God denouncing the pride of the king of Tyre. In verses 11-19, God expands His references to a "superhuman" being that most scholars believe to be Satan. Briefly describe Satan's unique privileges before his fall (verses 12-15).

Give an overview of Satan's judgment in verses 16-19.

What insights did you gain about pride that will help you resist it in your life?

Fact #2: God gives grace to the humble—Look at these scriptures and note the variety of ways "grace" is used and its source.

Ephesians 2:8—

Galatians 2:9—

2 Timothy 2:1—

How should the source of grace create humility in you?

Fact #3: God requires submission—Write out what Jesus says about obedience and submission.

John 14:15—

John 15:5-6—

John 15:10—

Jesus also spoke of divided interests or loyalties in Matthew 6:24-26. What is His message?

What does the apostle John have to say about divided interests in 1 John 2:15-17?

In Romans 6:17-18, how does Paul describe the person who is obedient and submissive to God?

Obedience or submission is not easy. In a few words, note the apostle Paul's struggle with obedience in Romans 7:19-23 and his frustration in verse 24.

How does Paul's struggle with obedience give you encouragement and instruction in your own struggles?

 Fact #4: God exalts the humble—Read Philippians 2:5-8 in your Bible and note the seven steps of humility. Then read Philippians 2:9-11 and record the ways the Father honors Jesus' humiliation, both past and future.

Verse 9—

Verse 10—

Verse 11—

Read James 4:7-10. Dr. Charles Ryrie points out, "There are 10 verbs, all commands, in these verses, in a tense which indicates the need for a decisive and urgent break with the old life."[1] Record your role and God's role according to James 4:10.

What can you decide to do to humble yourself to God's instructions and break with the old life?

Taking Steps Toward Humility

Scan the steps toward humility mentioned in this section of your book. Then list any of the suggestions you are willing to put into practice that would contribute to greater humility in you. Give specific situations and times when you'll do them.

Consult Scripture—

Pray—

Spend time with humble people—

Always take the low road—

Serve every person you meet—

Find the needy—

Refuse to talk about yourself—

Actively promote other people—

Moving Forward

Read this section in your book again. Write out the steps or actions you were asked to take to fulfill your desire to become a humble woman. Feel free to add any additional items to this list.

As you consider these steps, check the ones you will take today. What difference do you think moving forward on these steps will make in living out God's plan in a humble manner?

17

Looking for Contentment in All the Wrong Places

For the LORD God is a sun and shield;
the LORD will give grace and glory;
no good thing will He withhold
from those who walk uprightly.

PSALM 84:11

Read chapter 17, "Looking for Contentment in All the Wrong Places," in *Following God with All Your Heart*. Note any new truths or encouragements that motivate you to tackle what God is asking of you today.

What exciting opportunities are yours today as you seek to follow God? Jot them down and keep them in mind as you work your way through this exciting lesson on trusting God for His will and plan for your life.

4/13/11 - NO "CAT FRIENDLY" NEEDED NOW...

Hiding God's Word in Your Heart

Memorize Psalm 84:11. Write down how it appears in your favorite version of the Bible. You may want to look at a few other translations and note any words that differ to help you better understand the meaning of this powerful verse. What part of this verse really stands out and speaks to your heart today?

IF MY HEART IS ALWAYS WITH GOD, HE'LL ALWAYS BE WITH ME.

Traveling to God's Temple

Psalm 84 is a "pilgrim's" psalm recited by worshipers who traveled to Jerusalem to worship. Note the eager anticipation of those traveling to God's temple in:

Psalm 122:1-4—
REJOICING - EXCITED ABOUT CHANCE TO PRAISE GOD

Psalm 125:1-2—
TRUST, LORD WILL KEEP & SURROUND

Psalm 132:13-17—
ETERNAL BLESSING

Psalm 134:1-3—
PRAISE HIM & SERVE HIM

As you reflect on these psalms, what are your thoughts about your level of joyful anticipation, commitment, and devotion to church and worship?

Looking for a Contented Woman

Write out a dictionary definition for "contentment."

Now state this definition in your own words.

PEACEFULLY HAPPY WITH WHATEVER YOU HAVE.

Can you add your name to this statement made in your book?

All that _ELAINE_ needs is all that God is and all that He has already provided for _ELAINE_ in _ELAINE_'s present situation.

The Opposites of Contentment

Note how these men and women were blessed and the results of looking for contentment in all the wrong places.

Aaron and Miriam—brother and sister of Moses

Their blessed state (Micah 6:4)—

The issue (Numbers 12:1-2)—

The confrontation (verses 5-9)—

The consequences (verses 10-11)—

Achan—a soldier in Joshua's army

His blessed state—Achan was a victorious warrior who had a large family and possessed many herds.

The issue (Joshua 7:21)—

His choice and confession (verse 20)—

The consequences (verses 24-25)—

David—King of Israel

His blessed state (2 Samuel 8:15; 12:8)—

The issue (2 Samuel 11:2-3)—

The choice (verse 4)—

The consequences (2 Samuel 12:10-11)—

Persian leaders

> Their blessed state—These men were the top administrators over all of the officials of the kingdom of Darius, king of Persia (Daniel 6:2).

> The issue (verse 3)—

> The choice (verse 4)—

> The consequences (verse 24)—

List several insights you gain from all these examples.

Settling the Issue of Discontentment

Read Psalm 84:11 again. As you think about God's provision, write out a prayer to pray whenever a hint of discontentment creeps into your heart and mind. Include some elements of Psalm 84:11 or other verses that deal with contentment.

GOD GRANT ME THE SERENITY...

Turning the Corner to Contentment

Begin considering the reasons why you can be content.

WHY WORRY?!

Reason #1—God is a sun. Read these verses and note the blessings of having God as your "sun."

Psalm 30:5—

Hebrews 13:8—

2 Samuel 22:29—

Psalm 18:28-29—

MY LIGHT &, MY STRENGTH & MY PROTECTOR

✗ Malachi 4:2—

Psalm 30:11—

WAILING INTO DANCING...

Reason #2—God is a shield. Read these verses and note the blessings of having God as your "shield."

Psalm 3:1-5—

Psalm 5:11-12—

Psalm 28:7—

Psalm 33:18-20—

Moving Forward

Read this section in your book again. Write out the steps or actions you were asked to take to nurture contentment in your heart. Feel free to add any additional items to this list.

- PERSPECTIVE & UNDERSTANDING

As you consider these steps, check the ones you will take today. What difference do you think moving forward on these steps will make in living with contentment as you live out God's plan for you?

18

Living with Grace and Glory

For the LORD God is a sun and shield;
the LORD will give grace and glory;
no good thing will He withhold
from those who walk uprightly.

PSALM 84:11

 Read chapter 18, "Living with Grace and Glory," in *Following God with All Your Heart*. Note any new truths or encouragements that motivate you to tackle what God is asking of you today.

What exciting opportunities are yours today as you seek to follow God? Jot them down and keep them in mind as you work your way through this exciting lesson on trusting God for His will and plan for your life.

Hiding God's Word in Your Heart

Write out Psalm 84:11—from memory if you can.

Read these verses and write down what they teach about God's perspective on earthly goods.

Matthew 6:19-20—

Matthew 6:25-33—

Matthew 16:24-26—

Luke 12:16-21—

As you think about contentment and these truths, what perspective and attitude should you have toward the "stuff" you now have or want or might want in the future?

Reason #3—God gives us grace. Jot down a dictionary definition of "grace" as it applies to God's dealings with mankind.

What issues are you facing today that require God's grace?

As you look ahead, what issues might you face in the future that require God's grace?

Read 2 Corinthians 12:7-10 and note the apostle Paul's experience with his "issue" and God's grace. How does it encourage you?

What Does Grace Do?

In addition to the verses in your book, note further insights from these scriptures.

God's grace saves you.

2 Timothy 1:1 and 9—

Titus 3:7—

God's grace guides you.

Ephesians 3:8—

Ephesians 4:7—

God's grace empowers you.

Acts 4:33—

Ephesians 3:16—

God's grace is sufficient for you.

Hebrews 4:16—

Reason #4—God gives us glory. Summarize the meaning of "glory."

How does this nurture contentment in your heart?

Understanding God's Glory

God's glory is His awesome presence—Describe the overpowering presence of God's glory in these verses.

Exodus 24:16-17—

Exodus 40:34—

God's glory is a display of His nature—Which element of God's nature is described in these verses?

Job 25:3—

Psalm 19:1—

Psalm 24:8—

Psalm 29:2—

Psalm 104:31—

God's glory is displayed in Christ—How is God's glory through His Son described in these scriptures?

John 12:23—

John 17:1—

John 17:5—

John 17:24—

Reflecting God's Glory

Glance through this section of your book again. How do you respond to the idea that you are a reflection of God's glory?

Write a sentence or two about some changes you need to make to be a better "reflector" of the glory of God.

Moving Forward

Read this section in your book again. Write out the steps or actions you were asked to take to nurture contentment in your heart. Feel free to add any additional items to this list.

As you consider these steps, check the ones you will take today. What difference do you think moving forward on these steps will make in living with contentment as you live out God's plan for you?

19

Traveling the Road to Contentment

For the LORD God is a sun and shield;
the LORD will give grace and glory;
no good thing will He withhold
from those who walk uprightly.

PSALM 84:11

Read chapter 19, "Traveling the Road to Contentment," in *Following God with All Your Heart*. Note any new truths or encouragements that motivate you to tackle what God is asking of you today.

What exciting opportunities are yours today as you seek to follow God? Jot them down and keep them in mind as you work your way through this exciting lesson on trusting God for His will and plan for your life.

Hiding God's Word in Your Heart

Write out Psalm 84:11—from memory if you can.

Goals Versus Contentment

Scan the benefits of goals. What do you think about goals—are they a complement or irritant to contentment? Explain.

Do you have practical and spiritual goals? If not, when will you sit down and list some goals for the future? Name the day and time here and put it on your calendar as a "Retreat with God."

This SATURDAY!

Five More Reasons Why You Can Be Content

List the first four reasons for contentment.

#1 *I HAVE ENOUGH!*

#2 _____

#3 _____

#4 _____

Reason #5—God gives what is good. To understand what is truly "good," note what these verses teach about the goodness of God.

Exodus 34:6—

READY TO GIVE

Psalm 69:16—

WILL HAVE MERCY & WILL ANSWER US

Psalm 86:5—

Psalm 118:29—

LOVE ENDURES 4 EVER

Romans 2:4—

KIND TOLERANT & PATIENT

2 Thessalonians 1:11-12—

EVERY GOOD DESIRE - BE HONORED BY GOD

How can a better understanding of the goodness of God help you deal with your daily issues, responsibilities, and opportunities?

LESS WORRY & MORE PATIENCE - TRUST MORE

List one decision you need to make about a purchase, a relationship, or an opportunity.

FLORIDA!

PC 223

With that decision to be made in mind, write out the four test questions listed in your book and answer them.

1.

2.

3.

4.

What other spiritual resources might help you in making the best decision?

A Contentment Breakthrough

Describe a time when you experienced a breakthrough in the area of contentment. For instance, what did you desire or what did you think was missing in your life? What finally helped you to move forward to contentment?

Sources of Contentment

Contentment has its foundation in God—Are you struggling with an area of discontent? What have you learned from Psalm 84:11 about God that will help you to be content with what you have or don't have?

Contentment comes with focused devotion—If you are wrestling with discontent, ask, "Have I lost my focused devotion?" If so, what will you do to refocus on God?

CANNOT SERVE GOD & MAMMON

Contentment is a learned perspective—How does knowing that contentment is a learned perspective encourage you today?

SEEK YE FIRST...
✱ PHIL 4:12

Anything learned can also be forgotten. What can you do each day to remember God's promises to take complete care of you?

READ THE BIBLE...
GO THE TO SOURCE OF ALL THINGS!

REMEMBER THE PAST FIVE YRS!

COL 3:2 !

Moving Forward

Read this section in your book again. Write out the steps or actions you were asked to take to nurture contentment in your heart. Feel free to add any additional items to this list.

As you consider these steps, check the ones you will take today. What difference do you think moving forward on these steps will make in living with contentment as you live out God's plan for you?

20

Walking in Peace and Freedom

For the LORD God is a sun and shield;
the LORD will give grace and glory;
no good thing will He withhold
from those who walk uprightly.

PSALM 84:11

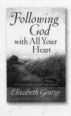

Read chapter 20, "Walking in Peace and Freedom," in *Following God with All Your Heart*. Note any new truths or encouragements that motivate you to tackle what God is asking of you today.

What exciting opportunities are yours today as you seek to follow God? Jot them down and keep them in mind as you work your way through this exciting lesson on trusting God for His will and plan for your life.

Hiding God's Word in Your Heart

Write out Psalm 84:11—from memory if you can.

Learning About God's Promises

Since any promise is only as valid as the one making it, how do these verses give you greater confidence in the promises given in Psalm 84:11?

Numbers 23:19—

GOD DOES NOT LIE OR CHANGE HIS MIND - HE KEEPS HIS PROMISES.

Psalm 100:5—

HIS LOVE & FAITHFULNESS ENDURES 4 EVER

Psalm 146:5-6—

LORD REMAINS FAITHFUL FOREVER

Hebrews 6:13-18—

GOD'S PROMISE IS SINCERE AND HE CANNOT LIE. UNCHANGING NATURE OF HIS PURPOSE.

> *"Immutable" was used in biblical times as a legal term describing the unchangeable nature of a will that could only be altered by the maker of the will.*

Receiving God's Promises

Look again at Psalm 84:11. What similar concepts of obedience and blessings are found in Psalm 34:8-10?

THOSE WHO FEAR GOD LACK NOTHING
SEE HIM & TAKE REFUGE IN HIM

Do you desire God's blessings? Then what does Psalm 84:11 say you must do?

WALK UPRIGHTLY.

Living Blamelessly

Read Acts 13:22, which includes God's commentary on David's life. As stated in your book, God was not describing "sinless perfection." What attitude did God point out about David that qualified him to be a man after God's own heart?

" HE WILL DO EVERYTHING THAT I WANT HIM TO DO "
FOLLOW GOD!

What connection do you see between heart attitude and blameless living?

Are there any messages being sent to your heart about your attitude or conduct? Any changes that need to be made?

LESS FEAR, MORE TRUST DAILY!

Watch Out for Sin

Read the account of the entrance of sin into the world in Genesis 3:1-13. Characterize the serpent (verse 1)—

Describe the progression of Eve's fall (verses 1-6)—

Note Adam and Eve's responses to God (verses 11-13)—

What insights can you gain from Eve's actions?

Now read about the progression of sin into the family unit in Genesis 4:1-9. What was Cain's problem (verses 1-5)?

What was God's caution (verse 6)?

What was Cain's response to God's concern (verse 8)?

In what way did Cain fail to take responsibility for his actions (verse 9)?

What lessons can you learn from Cain's interaction with God?

Read and reflect on these verses, noting God's guidelines for watching for and dealing with sin.

 Search for sin (Psalm 139:23-24)—Why do we hesitate at times to pray this psalm?

AFRAID OF GOD'S EXAMINATION OF US.

Acknowledge sin (Psalm 32:5)—Adam, Eve, and Cain did not want to admit their sin. Is there any sin you need to talk over with God?

YES.

Confess sin (Psalm 32:5; 1 John 1:9)—Confession is simply admitting something. Is there anything you need to admit to God? Do it now!

YES!

Receive forgiveness (Psalm 32:5 and 1)—Only God gives you a second chance. David rejoiced at his forgiveness, and you can too. Stop and praise God now for His marvelous grace!

Move on! (Psalm 32:8)—Has sin and failure kept you from pursuing or participating in an area of service to God and others? Once you have followed these guidelines, you can always move on and move forward. In fact, you must. It's part of living out God's plan for you. What steps are you going to take today?

> *32:8 I WILL INSTRUCT YOU PUT ONE FOOT IN FRONT*
> *AND TEACH YOU IN THE WAY OF THE OTHER*
> *YOU SHOULD GO. & TRUDGE!*

Confronting Sin in Real Life

Share a personal story about victory over sin and God's consequent blessings.

Practicing Your Priorities

Write out the message from these scriptures about priorities.

Your walk with the Lord.

Ephesians 4:14-15—

> *NO LONGER BE INFANTS, TOSSED TO & FRO*

2 Peter 3:17-18—

> *NOT BE CARRIED AWAY BY LAWLESSNESS*
> *NOT INFLUENCED BY THE WORLD*

Hebrews 5:12-14—

> *GOOD & EVIL DISCERNMENT*
> *AFTER PRACTICE OF UNDERSTANDING*

Your family.

Exodus 20:12; Ephesians 6:4—

HONOR PARENTS, HONOR CHILDREN
WITH LOVE OF GOD

Deuteronomy 6:6-9—

TEACH CHILDREN WELL

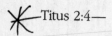—Titus 2:4—

Your home.

Proverbs 31:27—

SHE WATCHES OVER HOUSEHOLD

Your ministry.

Psalm 100:2—

Galatians 5:13—

✳ 5:14!

How should knowing your God-given priorities help with managing your life and planning your days? Be sure to note any areas that need change or improvement.

Moving Forward

Read this section in your book again. Write out the steps or actions you were asked to take to nurture contentment in your heart. Feel free to add any additional items to this list.

As you consider these steps, check the ones you will take today. What difference do you think moving forward on these steps will make in living with contentment as you live out God's plan for you?

21

Believing and Living God's Plan

I can do all things through
Christ who strengthens me.

PHILIPPIANS 4:13

Read chapter 21, "Believing and Living God's Plan," in *Following God with All Your Heart.* Note any new truths or encouragements that motivate you to tackle what God is asking of you today.

What exciting opportunities are yours today as you seek to follow God? Jot them down and keep them in mind as you work your way through this exciting lesson on trusting God for His will and plan for your life.

ONE FT IN FRONT THE OTHER!

Hiding God's Word in Your Heart

Memorize Philippians 4:13. Write down how it appears in your favorite version of the Bible. You may want to look at a few other translations and note any words that differ to help you better understand the meaning of this powerful verse. What part of this verse really stands out and speaks to your heart today?

ALL THINGS

Taking a Walk

As you've memorized the six key scriptures featured in this book, what have you learned about memorizing Scripture? For instance, how have you done it? Did you have a special method, place, or time when you actively learned the verses? When did you do your memory work? And when did you meditate on what you learned? How and how often did you review your verses? Take a minute to share about your new discipline.

JOSHUA 1:8
1:9

Hopefully you completed this exercise. If so, you have accomplished several things.

- ❧   Because you've taken the time to note how you memorized Scripture, you can pass it on to others.

❧ You can note your progress not only in cultivating this important life-changing spiritual discipline, but acknowledge a job well done and faithfully pursued.

❧ You can give God thanks and glory for His help, His Word, and His truths.

❧ Best of all, you now have these forever, empowering scriptures in your heart and mind. They are always with you, for your every need at any time and all the time. And no one can take them from you.

As we looked at the benefits gained as you become the woman God wants you to be, we highlighted six areas. Write out the six section titles of the types of women featured in this book.

1. Successful Joshua 1: 8

2. Courageous Joshua 1: 9

3. Exceptional Romans 12:2

4. Humility 1 Peter 5:5-6

5. Content Psalm 84:11

6. Strong Philippians 4:13

Understanding True Confidence

Look again at Philippians 4:13. List any challenges, issues, events, relationships, or opportunities where you need God's confidence right now.

Work!

Describe why you can look upon this verse as "the ultimate confidence builder."

Read Philippians 4:10-12 and describe Paul's uncertain lifestyle and what these experiences taught him.

In verse 13 Paul describes his source of confidence. With your pen in hand, interact with the following sets of words, definitions, and descriptions. Circle or underline anything that instructs or encourages you. Share your thoughts and discoveries.

"I can do"—to have the strength or to prevail or be able to accomplish something.

God has empowered me ...

"All things"—entirely, wholly.

all, not most, or some.

"Through Christ"—believers are infused with His power.

He and His sacrifice and pattern *established* *strengthens me*

"Strengthens"—to be given strength, to be empowered, to be infused with power.

Come, my burden is light

Using these descriptions, in your own words write out your version of this confidence-building verse.

It's easy!!

Since Christ is the source of your confidence, describe the importance of keeping your relationship with Him strong and vital. Also note any practices or actions that will help.

Prayer, reading, meditation.

Increasing Your Confidence

In your book you were asked to identify your fears, dreads, and challenges. As you look at Philippians 4:13, write your Number One challenge in the blank. You may want to do this for each of your "all things."

I can do all things, including

physical labor that taxes me

through Christ who strengthens me.

How does the message of this truth increase your confidence?

focuses my energies

Following God with All Your Heart

In a few words, summarize what you've learned from each of the promises and truths featured in this study.

God's promise of success (Joshua 1:8)—

God's promise of courage (Joshua 1:9)—
Do not be afraid. Fear is not of God.

God's promise of an exceptional life (Romans 12:2)—
Perfect will of God.

God's promise of humility (1 Peter 5:5-6)—
God resists the proud

God's promise of contentment (Psalm 84:11)—
No good thing will He withhold

God's promise of strength (Philippians 4:13)—
all things through Christ

Moving Forward

Read this section in your book again. Write out the steps or actions you were asked to take to nurture contentment in your heart. Feel free to add any additional items to this list.

As you consider these steps, check the ones you will take today. What difference do you think moving forward on these steps will make in living with contentment as you live out God's plan for you?

re-read the books, keep good notes

Notes

Chapter 3 — The Road to Success

1. Charles F. Pfeiffer and Everett F. Harrison, *The Wycliffe Bible Commentary* (Chicago: Moody Press, 1990), pp. 207-08.

Chapter 7 — Fighting Your Fears

1. M.R. DeHaan and Henry G. Bosch, *Our Daily Bread* (Grand Rapids, MI: Zondervan Publishing House, 1982), December 27.

Chapter 12 — Following God's Will

1. Sherwood Eliot Wirt and Kersten Beckstrom, *Topical Encyclopedia of Living Quotations* (Minneapolis: Bethany House Publishers, 1982), p. 93.

Chapter 16 — Walking the Less-Traveled Road of Humility

1. Charles Caldwell Ryrie, *The Ryrie Study Bible* (Chicago: Moody Press, 1978), p. 1861.

Personal Notes

Personal Notes

_____

_____

_____

_____

_____

_____

_____

_____

_____

_____

_____

_____

_____

_____

A Woman After God's Own Heart® Study Series

Bible Studies for Busy Women

God wrote the Bible to change hearts and lives. Every study in this series is written with that in mind—and is especially focused on helping Christian women know how God desires for them to live.

—Elizabeth George

Sharing wisdom gleaned from more than 20 years as a women's Bible study teacher, Elizabeth has prepared insightful lessons that can be completed in 15 to 20 minutes per day. Each lesson includes thought-provoking questions, insights, Bible-study tips, instructions for leading a discussion group, and a "heart response" section to make the Bible passage more personal.

Living with Passion and Purpose — LUKE — Elizabeth George
978-0-7369-0816-0

Becoming a Woman of Beauty & Strength — ESTHER — Elizabeth George
978-0-7369-0489-6

Putting On a Gentle & Quiet Spirit — I PETER — Elizabeth George
978-0-7369-0290-8

Discovering the Treasures of a Godly Woman — PROVERBS 31 — Elizabeth George
978-0-7369-0818-4

Nurturing a Heart of Humility — CHARACTER STUDIES MARY — Elizabeth George
978-0-7369-0300-4

Walking in God's Promises — CHARACTER STUDIES SARAH — Elizabeth George
978-0-7369-0301-1

Experiencing God's Peace — PHILIPPIANS — Elizabeth George
978-0-7369-0289-2

Pursuing Godliness — I TIMOTHY — Elizabeth George
978-0-7369-0665-4

Cultivating a Life of Character — JUDGES/RUTH — Elizabeth George
978-0-7369-0498-8

Growing in Wisdom & Faith — JAMES — Elizabeth George
978-0-7369-0490-2

HARVEST HOUSE PUBLISHERS
EUGENE, OREGON 97402
www.harvesthousepublishers.com

Books for a Teen Girl's Heart

⤳by Elizabeth George⤳

A Young Woman After God's Own Heart

How can you pursue God's heart every day? By understanding and following His plan for friendships, faith, family relationships, and your future. Elizabeth reveals how you can...

- enjoy more meaningful relationships
- make wise choices
- become spiritually strong

Join this exciting adventure of a lifetime—become a woman after God's own heart!

A Young Woman's Walk with God

Experience the love, joy, peace, patience, kindness, goodness, faithfulness, gentleness, and self-control Jesus possessed. Discover the fruit of the Spirit so you can...

- be positive as you interact with family and friends
- have peace regardless of school and relationship pressures
- experience joy even when facing difficulties

As you walk with Jesus your life will be more exciting and fulfilling in every way.

A Young Woman's Call to Prayer

God has given you an amazing gift— the ability to personally talk with Him every day! Through prayer, you can share with God your joys and triumphs, hurts and fears, and wants and needs, knowing that He cares about every detail. Elizabeth helps you...

- set a regular time to talk to Him
- share sticky situations and special concerns with Him
- discover and live His will

God is your forever friend—and He's always ready to talk with you!

A Young Woman After God's Own Heart—A Devotional

Can you believe that God wants to hear about your day and your dreams, worries, and hopes? It's amazing—and true! Elizabeth shares devotions to put you in touch with God and help you discover how to…

- live out your faith
- let go of your worries
- grow in beauty and confidence

Don't miss this incredible faith journey that will fill your life with joy and purpose.

Books by Elizabeth George

- Beautiful in God's Eyes
- Finding God's Path Through Your Trials
- Following God with All Your Heart
- Life Management for Busy Women
- Loving God with All Your Mind
- A Mom After God's Own Heart
- Powerful Promises for Every Woman
- The Remarkable Women of the Bible
- Small Changes for a Better Life
- Walking with the Women of the Bible
- A Wife After God's Own Heart
- A Woman After God's Own Heart®
- A Woman After God's Own Heart® Deluxe Edition
- A Woman After God's Own Heart®—A Daily Devotional
- A Woman After God's Own Heart® Collection
- A Woman's Call to Prayer
- A Woman's High Calling
- A Woman's Walk with God
- A Young Woman After God's Own Heart
- A Young Woman After God's Own Heart—A Devotional
- A Young Woman's Call to Prayer
- A Young Woman's Walk with God

Children's Books

- God's Wisdom for Little Girls
- A Little Girl After God's Own Heart

Study Guides

- Beautiful in God's Eyes Growth & Study Guide
- Finding God's Path Through Your Trials Growth & Study Guide
- Following God with All Your Heart Growth & Study Guide
- Life Management for Busy Women Growth & Study Guide
- Loving God with All Your Mind Growth & Study Guide
- A Mom After God's Own Heart Growth & Study Guide
- The Remarkable Women of the Bible Growth & Study Guide
- Small Changes for a Better Life Growth & Study Guide
- A Wife After God's Own Heart Growth & Study Guide
- A Woman After God's Own Heart® Growth & Study Guide
- A Woman's Call to Prayer Growth & Study Guide
- A Woman's High Calling Growth & Study Guide
- A Woman's Walk with God Growth & Study Guide

Books by Jim & Elizabeth George

- God Loves His Precious Children
- God's Wisdom for Little Boys
- A Little Boy After God's Own Heart

Books by Jim George

- The Bare Bones Bible™ Handbook
- The Bare Bones Bible™ Bios
- A Husband After God's Own Heart
- A Man After God's Own Heart
- The Remarkable Prayers of the Bible
- A Young Man After God's Own Heart

About the Author

Elizabeth George is a bestselling author who has more than 4.8 million books in print. She is a popular speaker at Christian women's events. Her passion is to teach the Bible in a way that changes women's lives. For information about Elizabeth's speaking ministry, to sign up for her mailings, or to purchase her books visit her website:

www.ElizabethGeorge.com